Foreword by Bruce Lindley

MOUNTAINS
Of
DESTINY

Stepping Into The Kingdom!

PAMELA A. SEGNERI

Mountains Of Destiny - Stepping Into The Kingdom

Copyright © 2022 - Pamela Segneri

All rights reserved. This book is protected by the copyright laws of Australia. This book may not be copied or reprinted for commercial gain or profit. The use of short quotations or occasional page copying for personal or group study is permitted and encouraged provided the source is acknowledged. Permission will be granted upon request. Unless otherwise identified, Scripture quotations are taken from the New American Standard Bible® NASB® Copyright © 1960, 1971, 1977, 1995, 2020 by The Lockman Foundation. Used by permission. All rights reserved. www.Lockman.org. Scripture quotations marked TPT are from The Passion Translation®. Copyright © 2017 by BroadStreet Publishing® Group, LLC. Used by permission. All rights reserved. thePassionTranslation.com. Scripture quotations marked NKJV are from The Holy Bible, New King James Version. Copyright © 1982 by Thomas Nelson, Inc. Used by permission. All rights reserved. www.thenkjvbible.com. THE MESSAGE: The Bible in Contemporary Language Copyright © 1993, 2002, 2018 by Eugene H. Peterson. All rights reserved. Used by permission of NavPress. Represented by Tyndale House Publishers. Emphasis with Scripture quotations is the author's own. Please note that Mountain Train Media's publishing style capitalizes certain pronouns in Scripture that refer to the Father, Son, and Holy Spirit, and may differ from some Bible publishers' styles. Take note that the name satan and related names are not capitalized. We choose not to acknowledge him, even to the point of violating grammatical rules.

Front Cover Art Image by Sylvia Tracy Busam. Title: Daniel 2:44 The Everlasting Kingdom

Published by Mountain Train Media
QLD, Australia
publishing@mountaintrainmedia.com.au
www.mountaintrainmedia.com.au

ISBN: 978-0-6453782-2-1

Dedication

I firstly dedicate this work to the Lord Jesus Christ for without whom none of this would have happened.

To my husband Paul whose encouragement and belief in me never wanes even when mine does. Although the books may credit me as the author none would be written without his love and support.

To my precious family, especially my grand children who are a source of great delight as I encourage them in their journey with Christ to take their mountains of destiny.

4 MOUNTAINS OF DESTINY

Acknowledgements

As with any project there have been many who have encouraged and assisted along the way.

I want to especially acknowledge the tireless work of my husband Paul, his editing and design skills have been a gift.

Thank you to my dear friends Bruce Lindley for writing the foreword and Sylvia Tracy Busam for her amazing prophetic artwork she has kindly allowed us to use on the cover of this book.

Thank you for your love and encouragement along the way.

6 MOUNTAINS OF DESTINY

Contents

Foreword: Bruce Lindley....p9

Introduction....p15

Chapter 1: Why Mountains?....p19

Chapter 2: Set High On A Hill....p29

Chapter 3: Mountains And The Fire Of God....p35

Chapter 4: Mountains Of Destiny And Elijah Fire....p39

Chapter 5: Mountain Moving Transformation....p45

Chapter 6: What Part Does Faith Play?....p47

Chapter 7: Mountains Will Shudder....p51

Chapter 8: Moving Into Your Mountain And Place Of Influence....p61

Chapter 9: It's Time To Go To The Mountain....p73

Chapter 10: Our Expectation - Victory....p79

Chapter 11: So What's My Mountain?....p85

Chapter 12: Mountain Moving Prayer....p93

Chapter 13: Who Am I In This....p101

Chapter 14: Why Do I Get To Talk About This?....p105

Chapter 15: From Here To There....p117

End Notes: p125

8 MOUNTAINS OF DESTINY

Foreword

Mountains of Destiny! What a great title for a book by Pamela Segneri. Why? Because we are created to do just that. Find our destiny and live it with purpose, authority and to transform our culture.

We are all created for a purpose. Not just any purpose – a divine purpose. A God destiny.

Fulfilment in life comes when you find your purpose and you live it. The good news is that it is never too late for you do this as there is no expiry date on your destiny.

Not just any destiny. God has created you for a divine destiny!

Jeremiah 29:11 says "For I know the plans I have for you," declares the Lord, "plans to prosper you and not to harm you, plans to give you hope and a future."

The key to life is finding your God given destiny. Regardless how culture defines "success", it is not just wealth, fame, lifelong relationships. No! It is finding God's destiny for your life and living it!

I've discovered that most Christians cannot articulate or define their God destiny. It is not just loving God or living a Christian life. It is much more specific than this - but it is not hard to discover. You only need to ask God and He will show you. The first step is to answer these few questions:-

"If you had unlimited time, opportunity, finance, what would you do for God?"

"What are you most passionate about changing in this world for Him?"

Just spend a moment now meditating and praying on these questions. Write down what comes to mind. Pray over it. What you have written typically is your God destiny.

This is very important but it is only the first step.

In order to live your destiny you have to do something!

You are called to move mountains and change the world.

Mountains are majestic. They can be beautiful to look at but they are also huge obstacles that have to be climbed or driven around for us to proceed in life.

Mountains are not just physical, they come in many shapes and forms. Some good and often bad.

Sometimes those mountains block our way forward in life and need to be moved. Jesus spoke about mountain moving faith in Mark 11:21-23. So it is possible to move those mountains that we encounter in life if we exercise our faith. Pamela will help you identify those mountains that need to need to move in your life and will show you how to move them.

There are other types of mountains in society today. Every culture has them – family, education, religion, business, government, arts/entertainment and media. These are foundational to every culture in the world. And most people work or aspire to succeed and even give the best years of their lives to immerse themselves in that mountain. They are the pillars, shapers and moulders of our society today.

But there is more!

The best definition of 'leadership' that I've heard is that leadership is 'influence'. The truth is that we all influence others' each day by what we say, how we live and especially what we do.

We all have 'spheres of influence' or a 'mountain' that we are called to shift, influence and live in with authority. In fact Jesus gave us all a mandate or a commission in Matthew 28:19-20 to 'go and make disciples of all nations.' The word 'nations' in the original Greek text is 'pante ethne' which translates to 'all people groups.' In other words, all diverse cultures.

Jesus has given us a mandate for all of us to 'go to the mountain of culture that we are called to transform for the kingdom of God.'

Pamela Segneri in 'Mountains of Destiny' powerfully unpacks Jesus' teaching in Matthew 5:13-15 that you are called to be the 'light of the world. A city set on a hill that cannot be hidden'.

When we were in Israel recently we not only visited where Jesus taught this text from his 'Sermon on the Mount' but we climbed the mountain opposite on the other side of the Sea of Galilee. It has a Roman city built on the top of that mountain called Hippos (also know as Susita). Hippos was one of the ten 'decapolis' cities that the Roman empire built throughout the middle east as they conquered new territories. They were all joined by the Roman Road. The ruins of this city on this mountain is still there today. Their goal was to transform the culture of every nation they conquered to the Roman culture.

Jesus knew that the people who heard him speak that day could see that city on the mountain in the distance as he told them they were called to be 'light of the world. A city set on a hill'.

This is our calling. The message of the gospel must influence all mountains of culture.

Get ready! You are about to be equipped and enlarged by "Mountains of Destiny"

Bruce Lindley
Co-Founding Apostle
ARC Global Apostolic Community
www.arcglobal.org

Introduction

Just as this book was being sent to the printers we have heard incredibly sad news for the nation, the commonwealth and in fact the rest of the world. Queen Elizabeth the second has left this mortal world and passed into glory.

I felt to include this in the introduction to this book as her life was well lived.

As we reflect on her life and reign as monarch we have to agree that she was one who faced her mountain of destiny with grace and courage. Her very real faith was the enabling factor in her courageous life.

She became the heir to the throne when her Uncle abdicated and her Father became King. In the natural it was thought that was not in the plan for her life. However, history will remember that she rose to the challenge for seventy years. A life time of service which I pray would inspire each one of us to accept the challenge of our destiny and rise to our place of destiny.

That we, like Queen Elizabeth, would have influence in the spheres God has called us to.

These are two quotes that I find both inspiring and

challenging and I pray they may inspire you also.

"If we are to better the future we must disturb the present." Catherine Booth (Co-Founder The Salvation Army)

"Don't downgrade your dream just to fit your reality, upgrade your convictions to match your destiny" Zig Ziglar

We are here in 2022 and I think it's safe to say the events of the last couple of years have indeed disturbed our present. The status quo has been shaken in a way we never expected — even though it had been prophesied many times that a great shaking was coming.

My position is the place we find ourselves in is not just a good place it is a great place. The proviso being that we don't retreat to the familiar, the comfortable.

Let me ask you, why did Sir Edmund Hilary[1] climb Mount Everest in 1953?

Why did Reinhold Messner[2] climb Mt Everest without supplemental oxygen in 1978 and then return in 1980 to make the first solo climb in that year.

There are so many others who have faced and conquered the geographical peaks.

The answer to the why for all of them is the mountains were there!

The question for us as we face our mountain sometimes in the valley of indecision - do I face down this thing or do I enjoy my quiet unremarkable life? The answer is of course the same - they are simply there and they are not moving of their own volition. As we progress through this journey you will find you have the authority to command them to move. It is entirely our call which challenge we conquer and which we simply tolerate.

I encourage you to be the hero of your own story. Don't stand on the side lines and spectate. Take heart from Joshua 1:6-7 & 9, 'Be strong and courageous,… be very strong and very courageous'. Knowing that as believers in the one true living God, He is with us in all things and His plan for each one of us is significant.

If you are unsure I pray this book will help you to find the answer, remembering Jesus is the way.

Let's go for our destiny!

CHAPTER 1

Why Mountains?

What Is the point of discussing mountains? I hear this question being asked in many situations both inside and outside the church. It reminds me of the inevitable stream of questioning voices that appear whenever there is a subject which is a little bit different being discussed.

Over the years those who know me best will attest to the fact that I have learned not to engage with every differing opinion.

Let me be clear on the answer. The Bible, which is my default position is full of mountains. God speaks prophetically of mountains in the Old Testament.

For right now I would ask that you stay with me, keep an open mind then search the scriptures for yourself with the guidance of Holy Spirit.

We know the language of scripture is often times symbolic or metaphorical, in the case of mountains in scripture I believe this is the truth.

Of course we are aware many remarkable and miraculous events were on actual mountains. Whilst acknowledging that, it is also true that if we search a little more we see mountains are representing High Spiritual Places. Perhaps our miracle is waiting as we go to that High Spiritual Place.

The most compelling reason for this study was that within our world there are many spheres of influence, mountains if you will. As I considered this, two thoughts materialised.

'Then God said, "Let Us make mankind in Our image, according to Our likeness; and let them rule over the fish of the sea and over the birds of the sky and over the livestock and over all the earth, and over every crawling thing that crawls on the earth." So God created man in His own image, in the image of God He created him; male and female He created them. God blessed them; and God said to them, "Be fruitful and multiply, and fill the earth, and subdue it; and rule over the fish of the sea and over the birds of the sky and over every living thing that moves on the earth."' Genesis 1:26-28 (NASB)

In this passage of scripture, God is speaking to His creation man (you and me). He tells us to rule, subdue and have dominion. I am not suggesting we have dominion over geological formations, however if God has given you a mandate for that then go for it. Mark 11:23 certainly could be read that way but please read it and every other scripture in context.

Many times the scripture says God will do this and we run off with our Word from God demanding it manifest, ignoring the truth that the equation is often incomplete. Please read the context. Let's be balanced in our application of the Word of God and in our lives, as a normal practice.

Please remember as we consider mountains or any other topic with Holy Spirit we should start to see the subject from God's perspective.

For instance as we consider love from God's perspective - unconditional love - which is only possible for us as we yield our mind, will and emotions to Him. Where we previously may have only seen shortcomings and sin we begin to see potential for righteousness.

In the same light as we gaze into His countenance and look at mountains from His perspective we no longer see obstacles and limitations, we begin to see miraculous possibilities. We can focus through his eyes and see the life of endless opportunities that the mountains open up to us.

Seeing our lives through the lens of heaven will cause us to develop a new mind set. This of course all comes back to the Word. In order to renew our minds, change our mindset we must start with new input. It's like uploading a new operating system and there are new features we must learn to get the most out of it.

In Romans 12:2, the scripture goes so far as to say we are transformed by the renewing of our minds.

And do not be conformed to this world, but be transformed by the renewing of your mind, so that you may prove what the will of God is, that which is good and acceptable and perfect.
Romans 12:2 (NASB)

Then suddenly, our mountains are possibilities, our failures become stepping stones to our success, our impossibilities become possibilities as we renew our minds with the Living Word.

Since the Bible talks a lot about mountains and many significant events happened on mountains it is wise to look into this a little more thoroughly.

Mountains have often been viewed as negative, as obstacles. Yet, I believe when you look at the weight of Biblical mountain references they are positive and supernatural. I began to consider that rather than being truly negative, obstacles are very cleverly used by the enemy to discourage us. It's too difficult, the price is too high and so on.

What Is A Mountain?

Well, a geological formation would be the considered response.

Lets dig a little deeper......

Bearing in mind the Bible language uses symbolism and we are basing our entire belief system on that Word, then surely it would make sense that we understand the meaning behind the meaning.

Our very good friends Adam F. Thompson and Adrian Beale wrote an extraordinary work aptly named *'The Divinity Code To Understanding Dreams and Visions'* and I would reference their revelation of mountains:

- Spiritual High Place
- Heaven
- Impossibility
- Obstacles
- Refuge / Hideaway

- Meeting place with God (God's Presence)
- Triumph
- Place of Prayer
- Place of Worship
- Place of Transformation
- Separation
- Ancient
- Apostolic Calling (Walking up mountain with Jesus)
- Seeing God's Glory (Top of the Mountain)
- God
- Doubt and Unbelief
- Pride

So with that as our frame of reference we look to our culture/society and those Mountains.

Right now as those mountain strongholds are held by secular/demonic forces who've made themselves right at home and in no way are they going to be deposed by us. It may seem daunting but that is the ploy of the enemy.

Please hear me on this, there are only two choices,

two sides, there is no Switzerland, no neutral zone in this life.

Not picking a side is indeed picking a side, right? We are called to stand up for righteousness.

So looking at mountains there is something about the human condition that relates back to Genesis. God says to Adam that he was to take dominion over the world around about him.

So as we look at our sphere of influence it is reasonable to propose that we are to take dominion over the circumstances. Consider for just a moment that we are the catalyst Holy Spirit has placed in this situation to shakeup the plans of the enemy. We need to start seeing ourselves in a different light, seeing ourselves as God sees us.

Let's try it, how often do we ask people how they are and they respond with 'Oh not bad under the circumstances'. I want to scream 'What are you doing under the circumstances?'. Let's start to see ourselves as the circumstance therefore whatever is going on around us must come into line with the Word of God.

That cannot simply be in a religious context. It has to be across the whole of society. We are the ecclesia, we are called to change culture.

It maybe challenging in the lives that we are living

sometimes to stand up for the things of God. Human beings like to be liked (some more than others) and if that's you it's horrible to be in that place whether at work, sports team, family or church, where you are standing alone.

My experience is there are usually others just waiting for someone to stand up.

I encourage you be that one. You will find the Hosts of Heaven will turn up and surround you.

I believe taking these Mountains of Influence for The Lord is exactly His plan for you and I - to go find our place on our particular mountain and stake our claim.

I believe the mountains that the world has raised up and glorified will be laid low by the power of the Living Christ, then God will raise up 'Glorious Mountains' in every sphere of influence.

These mountains are not harsh and inhospitable but the high places of God that He wants us to occupy and operate from, touching every part of humanity and playing an integral part drawing people into the ever expanding Kingdom of God.

"On Christ the solid rock I stand, when all around is sinking sand," (My Hope Is Built On Nothing Less chorus by Edward Mote 1834)

Those words should encourage us and remind us God is on the mountain.

CHAPTER 2

Set High On A Hill

At this point I would like to introduce Matthew chapter 5 through to chapter 7. This is the fundamental teaching of Christ and is extremely valuable in its entirety. There are 27 great doctrinal principles which Jesus presented at this time.

I particularly want to look at this scripture:

'You are the light of the world. A city set on a hill *(or mountain)* cannot be hidden.' Matthew 5:14 (NASB)

This is especially interesting as it is the first of these doctrines which Jesus held as fundamentally integral for us as believers.

So the first of these principles was influence. I'm not saying that this is more important than any of the other 26, I believe they are of equal importance. Our temple will not be built strong if we are missing any of the pillars.

However, what I am saying is that influence in our sphere is so important that Jesus noted it. We are to be a city set high on a hill - that's a place of influence, a place of recognition that those roundabout would easily see what is going on in our lives. Hill also maybe interpreted as mountain. Whether it's mountain or hill the point of this is that you are easily seen. You are not the undercover believers that so many have been for so many years.

Our commissioning in Mark 16:15-18 is to first go! Go be seen - let the world see who you are and what you stand for. Be the ecclesia - change the culture of your world.

> 'And He said to them, "Go into all the world and preach the gospel to all creation. The one who has believed and has been baptized will be saved; but the one who has not believed will be condemned. These signs will accompany those who have believed: in My name they will cast out demons, they will speak with new tongues; they will pick up serpents, and if they drink any deadly poison, it will not harm them; they will lay hands on the sick, and they will recover."'
> Mark 16:15-18 (NASB)

If it had not been important Jesus would not have said Go! In fact He may have even said stay, be safe. Don't rock the boat, don't upset people, don't upset the status quo. As we look at the life of Jesus and subsequently the lives of the apostles, they rocked people's worlds and because of that courage, bravery, that single focus of faith, that belief in Christ, we are here today.

We are not just here today, we are part of what God is doing in the earth forcefully advancing his kingdom and that is due to the influence we have in the situations and circumstances around us.

'You are the light of the world. A city set on a hill (or mountain) cannot be hidden.' Matthew 5:14 (NASB)

'Arise, shine; for your light has come, And the glory of the LORD has risen upon you.' Isaiah 60:1 (NASB)

'Nations will come to your light, And kings to the brightness of your rising.' Isaiah 60:3 (NASB)

We are the light of the world! When we are set in our proper place everyone can see, not just those who are close by. You can be seen from a great distance and therefore have more influence.

'Your attitude is changed by your altitude.'

As you stand in that higher place, that place of your destiny your perspective changes due to your altitude. In other words your attitude is changed by your altitude.

You are above the circumstances and trials that so often ensnare us.

'And the LORD will make you the head and not the tail, and you will only be above, and not be underneath, if you listen to the commandments of the LORD your God which I am commanding you today, to follow them carefully.' Deuteronomy 28:13 (NASB)

We are only above and not beneath in our predestined place, as we listen to and observe what God has commanded.

As we look from there we are looking from our place in the spirit realm so we can see the opposing demonic forces for what they are, like ants.

The further you go in the spirit the smaller they are!

I encourage you to seek God, get lost in Him and see how everything changes as you change.

As I have been writing this The Lord spoke a very simple word to me, it was very clear and there was an urgency about it.

He said, "Double up, double up, double up!".

He told me to decree it and I have been doing it everyday when Holy Spirit reminds me (which is often).

It was not about doubling up in any one area it was in every area.

As I make the decree different things come to me.

I notice there is much doubling up in the things of the Spirit, including a doubling of my intimacy with the Father. From that the practical and natural things flow and we have seen acceleration in many things, which is so exciting.

CHAPTER 3

Mountains And The Fire Of God

In order for us to step onto our mountain, our lane, our call, our mandate from God, there must be transformation within us. We can't step into a new enlarged sphere of influence without there first being a transformation. A transformation of our thinking and that of those around us; in and of ourselves we cannot do it. If we, as the church of Jesus Christ with our current programs could, we would have already done it!

We need to begin to operate differently,

> 'Moses gave us the Law, but Jesus the Anointed One, unveils truth wrapped in tender mercy.' John 1:17 (TPT)

When Jesus instructs us it kisses our hearts with mercy and truth.

Even as our sin is revealed, there is no pain in that correction, it draws us closer to Him.

The fires of purification are cleansing and redeeming - revealing our great need of our loving Saviour. They burn within us stoking the embers of devotion and passion, that cannot be faked.

'When Jesus instructs us it kisses our hearts with mercy and truth.'

Unlike man, when Jesus highlights sin it is never for the purpose of condemnation and punishment. It is always a call to redemption where we exchange the yoke of sin, guilt and shame for the yoke of divine union with Him. No adherence to religion or rules will ever change us.

We can act correctly, say the right things and behave in a way that makes us appear to be righteous but only our acceptance of the invitation to true repentance sets us free to receive the true gift of righteousness.

Fiery Arrows Vision

I had a vision many years ago, that I was in the room as Joash came to Elisha on his deathbed. The scene played out as in the scripture 2 Kings 13:14-19.

The major differences in the vision were the arrows were dipped in fire and the eastern window was looking to the East Coast of Australia.

As the arrows were fired I saw there was not just one man shooting there was a company of people. I believe spiritual warriors were shooting fiery arrows out to the eastern Australian seaboard. That vision was in 2013. In 2020 the East Coast of Australia caught fire

The Fire of God was and is reordering our nation bringing transformation to Australia and ultimately to the rest of the world.

This Time is the springboard into the most exciting days of our lives.

Yes, this is an era of increase, yes this is an era of promises being fulfilled in miraculous ways and yes this an era when Prophecies and decrees from the throne are manifesting!

Please note experientially I have found all of the above rarely occur without us playing our part. So what does that look like? For me it is less about doing and more about being! The promises of God seldom manifest in the way it played out in my head. However, the one thing I am sure of is God's way is so much better than I could have imagined. It is time to trust God completely, for some of us it is the first time, for others we have so easily shut God out (yet not necessarily deliberately) of different parts of our lives.

The question to each one of us is are you ready?

Are you ready to step up and play your part?

There are no spectators anymore we have to pick a side and be sold out to that.

There is an old saying, "There are three types of people. The first group make things happen, the second group watch things happen and then the third ask what happened?".

It's funny I know. My desire in sharing that is that each one of us is so intimate with The Lord that we only do what we see Him doing. We truly have become His hands and His feet on the Earth.

CHAPTER 4

Mountains of Destiny and Elijah Fire

We can't talk about Elijah Fire without mentioning a most exciting passage of scripture: 1 Kings 18:20, 1 Kings 19:1-3. In this passage of scripture Elijah climbed a personal mountain.

In 1 Kings 18:17-19 Elijah prophesied to Ahab exactly what was going to happen and it did. Why? Because the Fire of God fell!

Elijah secured a great victory in the name of the Lord, this wasn't simply a physical victory. There was also victory in the spirit realm, a realm we most certainly should be victoriously operating in today as we desire to transform our society and take the mountains. Elijah certainly began to scale that mountain.

Now here's Elijah standing up to the demonic forces mocking them telling them you, your buddy and the horse you rode in on be gone in the Name of the Lord because my God is the only one true God.

Not only did God miraculously answer with fire from heaven. He then told Elijah to kill the 400 prophets of Baal which he of course did in an exuberant fashion. This guy was sold out, obedient to the word of God and through him God did a complete work in that place.

At this point I want to examine the part of the story that is often just glossed over, what Elijah was doing as the prophets of Baal tried to invoke some sort of manifestation from their god.

In verse 30 of 1 Kings 18 we see Elijah repairing the altar of the Lord. The altar had previously been destroyed. The altar had been torn down as Israel had forsaken their covenant with the Lord God.

> 'Then Elijah said to all the people, "Come forward to me." So all the people came forward to him. And he repaired the altar of the LORD which had been torn down.' 1 Kings 18:20 (NASB)

We could draw a parallel with the church today and I will leave that up to you and Holy Spirit to see that correlation.

The bottom line was the altar had been destroyed and needed to be rebuilt. We need to rebuild the altar in our lives. We dare not stand before God and say well, the church I was in didn't build an altar/atmosphere of worship so it wasn't my fault. That's the disease of the modern day - it's no ones fault, yet "there is an anxious longing of the whole of creation waiting eagerly for the revealing of the sons of God." This is my paraphrase of Romans 8:19. The whole earth and everything in it is yearning for us to be who we are created to be; to be established in our destiny.

What happens next is interesting for us, after the victory Elijah warns Ahab of a great rain coming so Ahab quickly returns to Jezreel and reports all that has happened to his wife.

Then she (Jezebel), sends a message to Elijah - the spirit of Jezebel is characterised by accusation, intimidation and manipulation - and he receives it, bam!

Today I want us to make a decision and purpose not to receive that message.

Do not engage with demonic spirits. Block their numbers! Do not become Facebook friends or follow them on whatever - because that message sent Elijah running and he lost the plot.

He had just been instrumental in a huge victory however he listened to the accusation, was intimidated and manipulated by it. He was scared and ran, so the message is don't engage. Of course the enemy does not like losing ground, but we are more than overcomers', our victory is in Christ Jesus.

He has won so we can stand firm and because He has already won we have the privilege if we choose to operate from a place of victory.

That day everything could have completely changed in Israel. That day the culture/society of Israel could have been completely transformed but it took Jehu to ensure that.

So let's just recap Elijah's enormous victory over the prophets of Baal. He heard from God and he acted on it and the mountains in the form of religious opposition melted.

'The mountains melt like wax at the presence of the Lord, at the presence of the Lord of the whole earth.' Psalms 97:5 (NASB)

He, as we all know ran away and therefore did not complete the whole mission.

I want to encourage each one of us with the words of God to Joshua in Joshua 1 verses 6, 7 & 9. Be strong and courageous, Only be strong and very courageous, Be strong and courageous.

God commanded Joshua and I believe He is

charging us today with those very same words. I believe it is important to remember Our God, Our Loving Heavenly Father never sets us up for failure. If He is tasking us with a particular assignment in order to step into that place of destiny and influence, He has already seen the victory that we are predestined for.

We have to believe. Faith is the substance of things hoped for, the evidence of things not yet seen.

When we get that unction from God that is when our mountain moving Faith kicks in. We cannot yet see in the natural however, begin to see it in the sprit realm. Meditate on that put flesh on the bones of it and see it come to life.

> *"Be strong and courageous, for you shall give this people possession of the land which I swore to their fathers to give them. Only be strong and very courageous; be careful to do according to all the Law which Moses My servant commanded you; do not turn from it to the right or to the left, so that you may achieve success wherever you go. This Book of the Law shall not depart from your mouth, but you shall meditate on it day and night, so that you may be careful to do according to all that is written in it; for then you will make your way prosperous, and then you will achieve success. Have I not commanded you? Be strong and courageous!*

Do not be terrified nor dismayed, for the LORD your God is with you wherever you go." Joshua 1:6-9 *(NASB)*

CHAPTER 5

Mountain Moving Transformation

We often cite Caleb who as an 85 year old said give me my mountain. His confession in Joshua 14:11 was, "I am still as strong today as I was when Moses sent me out". That statement demonstrates he had the Fire of God burning passionately within him.

He knew that to take the mountain, he would have to depose those who were living there.

When you think of your mountain are you as strong as you were? Or are we living in past glories?

Can you visualise the victory even before you start?

Are you prepared to depose those who have taken up residence there?

This is not a time to co-exist with demons, dragons, or giants. Our call is to victory, personally and corporately.

One more thing to think about before we leave Caleb. His daughter Achsah, had married and been given land and then she came back to ask for a blessing from her Father. Blessing, birthright, inheritance is culturally associated with sons and here is this girl saying you've given me land now give me a blessing, give me springs of water.

Now what Caleb did was change culture. He blessed her as she asked and gave her the upper and the lower springs.

David slaying Goliath (1 Samuel 17) and Esther standing before Ahasuerus (Esther 1-2) both brought victory and transformation.

What is standing before you? It must yield to the authority you have in Christ. Therefore it is paramount that you cultivate your relationship with Jesus Christ.

When we take our mountain, culture must change. We are agents of transformation.

Transformation will lead to the 'Zoe' kind of life, the God kind of life we all desire.

CHAPTER 6

What Part Does Faith Play?

That is a truly valid question. I believe we can never underplay the importance of Faith. In fact, my personal opinion is that it's our Faith in the Lord Jesus Christ, who is the Living Word that moves mountains. He through our Faith undergirds every step we take as we travel this journey.

If Faith doesn't play that singular part in our life as believers, what are we believing in? Are we trusting in ourselves and our own ability to conquer mountains? If so, we may have a measure of progress. However, that is nothing like what we can achieve as we place our Faith in Christ. The other major downside is when you are doing things in your own strength you don't experience the ease of being in the flow from the throne of God.

Who can go up to the mountain of the Lord but he who has clean hands and a pure heart.

If you are a believer in Jesus Christ that's already you, our role now is to cultivate it further and protect that reality.

> 'And Jesus answered and said to them, "Have faith in God. Truly I say to you, whoever says to this mountain, 'Be taken up and thrown into the sea,' and does not doubt in his heart, but believes that what he says is going to happen, it will be granted to him. Therefore, I say to you, all things for which you pray and ask, believe that you have received them, and they will be granted to you.' Mark 11:22-24 (NASB)

It's not called Mountain moving Faith for nothing.

We must come to this place by revelation alone. No one can drum it into us. Often we need to hear the same thing said differently several times and then the light goes on.

It is wonderful to realise God is the giver of every good and perfect gift.

> 'Now to Him who is able to do far more abundantly beyond all that we ask or think, according to the power that works within us.' Ephesians 3:20 (NASB)

Exceedingly abundantly more than we can ask. He wants bless, prosper and protect us more than we even want or expect.

Everything we would desire in God, every promise the Word contains, every prophetic word we have received all have one thing in common. They are all activated by our Faith in the Lord.

So what part does Faith play? Every part, it is essential for our life journey with Christ.

CHAPTER 7

Mountains Will Shudder

This is our prophetic word for this time Isaiah 64:1-4.

"Oh, that You would rend the heavens! That You would come down! That the mountains might shake at Your presence— As fire burns brushwood, As fire causes water to boil— To make Your name known to Your adversaries, That the nations may tremble at Your presence! When You did awesome things for which we did not look, You came down, The mountains shook at Your presence. For since the beginning of the world Men have not heard nor perceived by the ear, Nor has the eye seen any God besides You, Who acts for the one who waits for Him."
(NKJV)

All the mountains will shudder before the Lord and

John 14:20 says we are in Him as He is in us, therefore it is not prideful or arrogant to believe that they will shudder before us.

Ephesians 3:20 says God is able to do exceedingly abundantly more than we can ask or hope for According to the power (of the Holy Spirit) which is at work within us. As we move in the authority of heaven, yes we speak and our words have power. I believe there is something deeper and more significant.

So what causes these great monoliths in our lives to shudder?

The answer is altogether too simple, it is Christ in us!

Jesus gave us His authority!

'And He called the twelve together, and gave them power and authority over all the demons and to heal diseases.' Luke 9:1 (NASB)

'The seventy returned with joy, saying, "Lord, even the demons are subject to us in Your name." And He said to them, "I was watching Satan fall from heaven like lightning. Behold, I have given you authority to tread on serpents and scorpions, and over all the power of the enemy, and nothing will injure you.' Luke 10:17-19 (NSAB)

He gave His authority to His disciples. Power over all the works of the enemy. The only question that remains is, are we His disciples? Or are we just going along for the ride and seeing how it turns out?

I love Psalms 103:20.

'Bless the LORD, you His angels, Mighty in strength, who perform His word, Obeying the voice of His word!' (NASB)

That says to me the angels are waiting, waiting for us His disciples, believers in Him and His word to speak the word that is within us. It is at that point the angels go to work. Be careful to note it is His word that accomplishes what it is sent to do, not our word. The angels obey the voice of His Word. As we speak out His Word the angels are moved into action.

So once again we need to get more intimate with God, allowing Holy Spirit to direct us to those areas that may need a little more attention, and letting Him flood us with Fire, Glory, Love whatever is necessary for us to stand before mountains fearless in our God given authority and watch them melt like wax!

To that end sometime ago the Lord told us to not facilitate conferences, rather they are to be a convergence. When we converge we all get on the same page, get our ducks are in a row as it were. And we have purpose, a singular purpose, divergently expressed perhaps but one purpose to see Christ preached and disciples made and the kingdom extended. In other words take the mountains.

Let's just go back to the Mountains. These are representative of our cultures and society, spheres of influence if you like;

>   Religion
>   Family
>   Government
>   Education
>   Arts and Entertainment
>   Media
>   Business

We all are in at least one of these which are you? You must know that in order to be effective. We either leave an impress on our culture or it will leave one on us.

We are called to be snipers not shotguns. Our aim must be deliberate, strategic and if you are not sure of your mountains you may just be out for a hike or camping.

Please hear me I am not saying in order to be fulfilling your destiny in the Government mountain you must be the President or Prime Minister, that is only true if you are called to it. You maybe called as a lobbyist, or a lawyer. Being at the top doesn't always mean you're successful if you are not called to it.

As in every area, Media doesn't mean you're going to be the next Rupert Murdoch or Mark Zuckerberg, it may mean you are called to hold them to account in wisdom and love. Let God speak to you about your place. It's important to know your lane and stay in it!

And in all these things that will pass away know this:

> You are a son of God,
> You are loved by Him,
> You have an eternal inheritance in Him.

He desires you would be in health and prosper even as your soul prospers (see John 3:2).

When we step into our proper place the mountains, society, culture around about us will shudder and tremble. Not because we just turned up, rather when we arrive we are accompanied by the hosts of heaven and we are the voice of His Word which the angels are charged to obey (see Psalms 103:20).

What I desire for each one of you is that you work with Holy Spirit to fulfil your destiny, step up onto your mountain and take it.

Ezekiel 36

As I look at Ezekiel 36 in my Bible the heading

reads 'The Mountains of Israel to Be Blessed'.

As I read that word I see not simply a geographic Israel but Spiritual Israel. That is to say I see the Church of Jesus Christ, us the believers in every mountain of society. It is indeed a big call. However, we have a much bigger God.

Imagine for a moment every mountain of culture/society completely under the Lordship of Jesus Christ. Now that would be a world we would all like to live in. Divine hope for the future would be present everyday in every way. Certainly we would call that blessing.

This scripture acknowledges that we have been reviled and endured criticism and insults and from verse 7 it turns around that those who have levelled insults and criticism will themselves have to endure those things.

And in verse 8, we the mountains of the Lord will put forth branches and bear fruit. So as we expand into that which we are called to, great blessing will come. Both, I believe in the form of people coming into the kingdom and wealth to the level God has pre ordained for each of us.

Verse 9 - God reminds us He is for us and He will cultivate and sow into us.

Verse 10 - He will multiply men to us. In other

words our influence will increase.

Verse 12 - God says this is our inheritance and as the the mountains flourish our influence increases.

At this point I would encourage you to meditate on that word and allow God to speak His wonders to you.

Influence Versus Dominion

Is there a difference?

Genesis 1:26-28 encourages us to have dominion over pretty much everything. Adam and Eve did not have any idea what they had until they lost it.

Since then we - mankind have been trying to exert our dominion/influence over the powers of spiritual darkness with varying degrees of success.

The real loss was not necessarily loss over birds and fish and animals, it was loss of dominion over those spiritual forces that war against the Spirit of God that is within us.

The enemy has always been in a battle for us.

I propose that the battle was and is for believers and non believers alike.

That is why Jesus Himself commanded us in Mark 16:15-18 to go.......

In verse 17, those who have believed in His name will cast out demons. That is also fulfilling Isaiah 61:1

'The Spirit of the Lord GOD is upon me, Because the LORD anointed me To bring good news to the humble; He has sent me to bind up the brokenhearted, To proclaim release to captives And freedom to prisoners' (NASB)

In Matthew 28:18-19 is Matthew's account of the Great Commission. Jesus began with, *"All authority is given to Me in heaven and on the earth."* Then the command to go. In the gospel of Matthew the transfer of authority is implied. The authority Jesus is speaking of is therefore given to us His disciples, since clearly He is going to Heaven and is addressing those who are left behind to carry on HIs work.

Why is that important enough for Jesus to mention in His last conversation before going back to His Father in heaven? Because this was always what it was about.

Adam and Eve gave their dominion/influence away and now the sleeping giant which is the church, the body of Christ must awaken and arise and shine. We need the authority of heaven. This authority we must learn to exercise with love, grace and mercy.

Dominion however, is adversarial and often times characterised by conflict, regardless, sometimes it has to be that way. An enemy who has held certain ground for generations is not simply going to go because you want it to or you asked nicely.

Influence is far more finessed.

> The Oxford Dictionary defines it as the capacity to have an effect on the character, development, or behaviour of someone or something, or the effect itself: the influence of television violence | I was still under the influence of my parents | [count noun] : their friends are having a bad influence on them.
> • the power to shape policy or ensure favourable treatment from someone, especially through status, contacts, or wealth: the institute has considerable influence with teachers.
> • [count noun] a person or thing with the capacity to have an influence on someone or something: Fiona was a good influence on her.
> 2 Physics, archaic electrical or magnetic induction.
> verb [with object] have an influence on: government regulations can influence behaviour, but often without changing underlying values and motivations.

As we look at the definitions and uses of influence we should realise how important it is that our influence as believers increases across all the mountains of culture.

Suffice to say if we are not influencing something/someone for good, then it or they are being influenced by and for evil.

The battle lines are clearly drawn there is only good and evil. There is no third option. Grey is mixture any level of evil is still evil. We need to see in black and white, knowing who our enemy is. Our enemy most certainly is not people as we are called to have great compassion for people who are being misled. Jesus wept over Jerusalem out of compassion, He never excused sin.

An important note;

You cannot influence a person or situation if you are the same. In that case you can only agree!

CHAPTER 8

Moving Into Your Mountain And Place Of Influence

Have you ever considered your walk with Christ and then thought, 'is this it?'

Is there more that I am not currently experiencing and walking in? And if so what is it?

Have you ever pondered? We are called to be Kings and Priests (Revelation 1:6, 5:10, 1 Peter 2:9) a royal priesthood. On reading these scriptures we may think intellectually "I know these things however, that is not my current reality".

If you can relate to any of the aforementioned questions it's time to press in. Also think about those you have in your sphere of influence as they maybe asking those very same questions.

Let's look at the Seven Mountains of Culture not as a doctrine but rather as a revelation.

The Religion Mountain is one mountain, just one in the mountain range of our society. Christ alone is over all, so whether our sphere of influence is religion, government, education, entertainment in its many expressions, media, family or business mountains we are called to release our God given gifting in that arena.

As we mature in our walk with Christ we develop more wisdom, we gain spiritual and secular authority. We may eventually sit in a place of government/influence within the sphere which God has already prepared for us, bearing in mind it is always entirely up to us.

This is prophetic promise which is simply an invitation from The Father to co-labour with Him.

As we look at the Word it would seem there are three levels of our walk.

> 'Blessed is the person who does not walk in the counsel of the wicked, Nor stand in the path of sinners, Nor sit in the seat of scoffers! But his delight is in the Law of the LORD, And on His Law he meditates day and night. He will be like a tree planted by streams of water, Which yields its fruit in its season, And its leaf does not

wither; And in whatever he does, he prospers.'
Psalms 1:1-3

Verse 1 - Realm of the Anointing, where we see clearly and make God choices.

Verse 2 - Realm of Authority, understanding and meditating on the Word of God which develops wisdom leading to authority.

Verse 3 - Seat of Government or Throne, firmly established and prospering in your place and therefore governing.

You can stay on any of those levels. For so long we have been encouraged to go after the anointing and that was enough. Please understand me, I love the flow of the anointing in my life and the lives of others but there is more, so much more. So I guess the next question is how do we get there?

The progression is interesting to me as the entry level in verse one is anointing. Unfortunately for many we have never been encouraged to progress past that. Just as anointing is not authority it is not influence.

In other words, you may move in the anointing exercising one or more or the gifts of the Holy Spirit and yet have no more influence than in that moment of connection.

The short answer is the character of Christ is not

yet formed within us. In order to move in any level of authority and subsequently government the character of Christ must be formed in us and that takes discipleship. A yielding, an apprenticeship to Christ if you will.

There is an old saying that goes 'your gift (anointing) may take you where your character won't keep you.' Now I love the anointing, I love the Holy Spirit moving in any and every circumstance but I want the measure of anointing to be enhanced by developed character, as I move in the Authority and government that is my portion. That will always increase our influence.

Looking at the life of David as a shepherd boy he was anointed by the Prophet Samuel at the direction of God.

He then moved on to authority at Hebron in 2 Samuel 5:3-4.

From authority to the throne in Jerusalem in 2 Samuel 5:6-7 when he overcame the Jebusites and that produced blessing and breakthrough.

Anointing

As we generally understand the anointing realm it is about gifting and the Holy Spirit flow of that gift.

'In that day the Lord will remove the heavy burden from your shoulders and break off the yoke of bondage from your necks because of the heavy anointing upon you!' Isaiah 10:27 (TPT)

Under heat or pressure oil is produced. 1 Corinthians 1:21-22 and 1 John 2:20 are the result of a gift from Holy Spirit.

If an increase in anointing is desired we would be wise to increase our praying in tongues and as the Holy Spirit leads fasting, to disencumber ourselves from whatever may be standing in our way.

We have all desired, celebrated and/or applauded the anointing and many have stopped there. They haven't gone on after Authority.

Authority

Authority is different this is what moves mountains!

Authority comes as a result of alignment. Who are we aligned with? Disciples received authority because they were aligned with Christ. If the level of our authority is not where it should be the question we must continually ask ourselves is am I aligned with Christ on this? (see Ephesians 4:11-12, Hebrews 7, Matthew 10:1-10, Luke 10:17).

2 Corinthians 10:12-16 illustrates Paul's heart

was to see his dimension of authority enlarged and extended. The Kingdom of God is ever increasing. It is doubtful that there is a problem or circumstance which an increase of the true authority heaven wouldn't solve.

If we carry a realm of authority in the Spirit it should be evident in the natural transformation of culture.

We witness many times in the life and ministry of Jesus. If we are willing to agree with Jesus He will move.

Spiritual Authority will shift things in culture and that is the Apostolic Call.

A) Paul tries to establish his measure of rule (Acts 16:6-10). So it is very important that we do not go into areas that God doesn't want us to be in as it causes problems (see v10).

B) Solomon used it to set boundaries (1 Kings 2:36-46). David warned him against a rebellious spirit and Solomon set the boundaries. It is key when dealing with a rebellious spirit.

C) God measures it out and allows us to grow into it. Ezekiel 47:3-5 shows an ever increasing area of influence. Whatever we are trusted with we need to grow into it.

D) My call in God determines my measurement of rule (1 Corinthians 15:10, Colossians 4:17).

E) Faithfulness determines my measurement of rule. (Luke 16:10-12, we need to serve someone else vision in order to fulfil our own).

F) Conquest not tenure produces measurement of rule. (2 Corinthians 2:6, battles fought and won give me authority to increase.)

Alignment

Alignment creates empowerment (Ephesians 4:11-12, covering creates control, alignment offers protection.)

Revelation shows you who someone is, not simply who they want you to see.

We choose to honour and we can show that honour in many ways through faithfulness, loyalty and obedience to the the Word. We can also show honour through finances, which we will look at a little later. A well used phrase is Sow where you want to go! In other words support someone else's vision Support someone else's vision.

Unity and Keeping rank. In Psalms 133 notice blessing was commanded on Zion not unity. The Father will never command unity. In saying that, God most certainly would desire for us to be in one accord,

He gave us free will. When we discover the joy and peace of unity then the spiritual dimension of the oil of anointing/blessing flows down Zechariah 4:12.

Body anointing/authority produces new dimensions (Ephesians 1:23). We know in the natural, physical realm to experience wellbeing the whole body must be well. Therefore the body of Christ in unity is much more effective than we are on our own. Every joint supplying, for us as human beings this is not necessarily something that comes easily. However, when we discover that we are indeed better together the anointing and authority increase exponentially. (Deuteronomy 32:30, Leviticus 26:8)

Finances are critical, Matthew 25:21 relates the parable of the talents. While a talent was a unit of currency they were rewarded in authority not just money which we can translate into finance. While money is a finite commodity our authority in the kingdom is infinite. We can always create wealth, we are told that in Deuteronomy 8:18. As we read that scripture it is interesting to note the Lord gives us the power to create wealth for no other reason than to confirm His covenant with us, which He swore to our Fathers Abraham, Isaac and Jacob. Important to note we should never chase money. Proverbs 23:5 says if we do it will sprout wings and fly away. Abram did obey God. However, God did not command Abram to honour Melchizedek with a tenth. Abram honoured Melchizedek of his freewill as he was the High priest of God. Honouring him would be accepted as honouring God. In Genesis 14:17-24, scripture records the great increase of his wealth, authority, influence in the land.

In Nehemiah 2:7-8 the King gave Nehemiah letters of passage/authority. When we have that authority from our King demonic forces must let us pass. Letters of provision so that like Nehemiah we will have all that we need to fulfil our call. The thing about finance is how much do you trust God?

Throne Or Seat Of Government

Sitting on a throne is the result of overcoming Proverbs 20:8. In 2 Kings 2:9-12 especially verse 12, under every powerful mantle there is a ripped garment that is the evidence of the overcoming that has taken place. Elijah's ministry as powerful as it had been, was now finished. Elisha had to forge a new way forward hence the ripping of the old way.

The Spirit of Elijah that is emerging now is not about one person but a company of people. That is the new way!

Remember the Spirit gives as He wills not as we do. So He is giving in every sphere of influence as the body of Christ, the sons of God yield to His will through His Spirit.

Lets have a look at Matthew 7:2-23.

'For in the way you judge, you will be judged; and by your standard of measure, it will be measured to you. Why do you look at the speck that is in your brother's eye, but do not notice the log that is in your own eye? Or how can you say to your brother, 'Let me take the speck out of your eye,' and look, the log is in your own eye? You hypocrite, first take the log out of your own eye, and then you will see clearly to take the speck out of your brother's eye! "Do not give what is holy to dogs, and do not throw your pearls before pigs, or they will trample them under their feet, and turn and tear you to pieces. "Ask, and it will be given to you; seek, and you will find; knock, and it will be opened to you. For everyone who asks receives, and the one who seeks finds, and to the one who knocks it will be opened. Or what person is there among you who, when his son asks for a loaf of bread, will give him a stone? Or if he asks for a fish, he will not give him a snake, will he? So if you, despite being evil, know how to give good gifts to your children, how much more will your Father who is in heaven give good things to those who ask Him! "In everything, therefore, treat people the

same way you want them to treat you, for this is the Law and the Prophets. "*Enter through the narrow gate; for the gate is wide and the way is broad that leads to destruction, and there are many who enter through it. For the gate is narrow and the way is constricted that leads to life, and there are few who find it.* "*Beware of the false prophets, who come to you in sheep's clothing, but inwardly are ravenous wolves. You will know them by their fruits. Grapes are not gathered from thorn bushes, nor figs from thistles, are they? So every good tree bears good fruit, but the bad tree bears bad fruit. A good tree cannot bear bad fruit, nor can a bad tree bear good fruit. Every tree that does not bear good fruit is cut down and thrown into the fire. So then, you will know them by their fruits.* "*Not everyone who says to Me, 'Lord, Lord,' will enter the kingdom of heaven, but the one who does the will of My Father who is in heaven will enter. Many will say to Me on that day, 'Lord, Lord, did we not prophesy in Your name, and in Your name cast out demons, and in Your name perform many miracles?' And then I will declare to them, 'I never knew you; LEAVE ME, YOU WHO PRACTICE LAWLESSNESS.'"*
(NASB)

What this passage says to us is we may function

in a gifting and be cast out …. But not if we are in authority/alignment/s then…..

It's Time For Us To Go To The Mountain!

CHAPTER 9

IT'S TIME TO GO TO THE MOUNTAIN

This is now the time to consider those things that have kept us from taking our place on the mountain of society/culture to which God has predestined for us.

'At the bottom of the mountain, they were met by a crowd of waiting people. As they approached, a man came out of the crowd and fell to his knees begging, "Master, have mercy on my son. He goes out of his mind and suffers terribly, falling into seizures. Frequently he is pitched into the fire, other times into the river. I brought him to your disciples, but they could do nothing for him." Jesus said, "What a generation! No sense of God! No focus to your *lives! How many times do I have to go over these things? How much longer do I have to put up with this? Bring the boy here." He ordered the afflicting demon out—and it was out, gone. From that moment on the boy was well. When the disciples had Jesus off to themselves, they asked, "Why couldn't we throw it out?" "Because you're not yet taking God seriously," said Jesus. "The simple truth is that if you had a mere kernel of faith, a poppy seed, say, you would tell this mountain, 'Move!' and it would move. There is nothing you wouldn't be able to tackle."' Matthew 17:14-20* (MSG)

Unfortunately there are so many standing around yelling at the mountain to move but as Jesus said 'You are not yet taking God seriously'

We are all familiar with this scripture and I'm sure we've stood before our personal mountain and done precisely that. Surprise mountain has remained. Perhaps sometimes diminished in size somewhat but not moved out of our lives as the infallible word of God tells us. Since there is no fault with God we must have missed something.

'The mountains take one look at GOD And melt, melt like wax before earth's Lord. The heavens announce that he'll set everything right, And everyone will see it happen—glorious! All who

> serve handcrafted gods will be sorry— And they were so proud of their ragamuffin gods! On your knees, all you gods—worship him! And Zion, you listen and take heart! Daughters of Zion, sing your hearts out: GOD has done it all, has set everything right. You, GOD, are High God of the cosmos, Far, far higher than any of the gods. GOD loves all who hate evil, And those who love him he keeps safe, Snatches them from the grip of the wicked. Light-seeds are planted in the souls of God's people, Joy-seeds are planted in good heart-soil. So, God's people, shout praise to GOD, Give thanks to our Holy God!' Psalms 97:5-12 (MSG)

The mountains melt like wax!

We all know what that's like we've all watched a candle melt down.

> 'The mountains melt like wax at the presence of the LORD, At the presence of the Lord of the whole earth.' Psalms 97:5 (NKJV)

The Mountains melt at the presence of the Lord. So my responsibility is to spend time in His presence.

> 'The mountains will melt under Him And the valleys will be split, Like wax before the fire, Like water poured down a steep place.' Micah 1:4 (NASB)

Now God's not coming out of heaven to melt your mountain - shock!

Of course He's not! Why? Because He already did.

That's why we praise and worship, God presences Himself in the praises of His people. In the gospel of John 15:16-23 it talks about the Lord abiding with us and in us. Since we know that God said it and He is not a man that He would lie, the truth is He is in us and with us. Our role in this is to cultivate His presence.

I have had a long held dream that as people looked at me it would be the Lord they saw. Therefore; as we stand before these mountains, the mountains, the obstacles, the principalities and powers would see The Lord. They would do according to the Word - shudder and melt.

We praise because He is with us, God is there when we confront our mountain and it must go!

The scriptures we've read tell us there is nothing that can stand before the presence of the Lord God.

The more we read scripture, meditate and praise not just in church but more importantly in our own time God will inhabit our praises.

Clearly put, He infills us with His Divine Authority. Our faith level then becomes indomitable and the long yearned for transformation happens before our eyes.

Just in case you need further convincing;

> 'Behold, I have given you authority to walk on snakes and scorpions, and authority over all the power of the enemy, and nothing will injure you.' Luke 10:19 (NASB)

Let's look at some of those mountains, those things that restrict our lives and hold us in containment. Those things that Jesus' death and resurrection bought freedom for us.

- Sickness
- Poverty
- Addictions
- Bondages
- Loneliness
- Unforgiveness/Bitterness/Resentment
- Envy
- Pride
- Anger
- Rejection
- Grief/Loss

It doesn't matter what your mountain or mountains are, you must apply the presence of God to them and they will go.

To do that successfully we must live in the presence.

He's in us but let Him show. Don't just put Him on like an overcoat, what's that line? Don't leave home without Him!

If we can master this the enemy will never ensnare us again, we can move on and live for Christ and truly fulfil our purpose and destiny.

CHAPTER 10

Our Expectation - Victory

God is for us, that is an absolute truth. It is more than reasonable when we speak, sing and prophesy of our love and devotion to Him that we would actually believe Him.

So looking at Isaiah 64:3

> 'When You did awesome things which we did not expect, You came down, the mountains quaked at Your presence.' (NASB)

Even though the children of Israel did not expect - God in His kindness and mercy still did amazing things.

We have a far superior covenant cut with the Blood of Jesus therefore, we should expect great and awesome things. That is why as we read of the mountains quaking at His presence, and if the mountains we are going after aren't moving the fault is never with God.

We are a generation that has more revelation across the body than ever before. Haggai says several times "consider your ways". Now I guess mainly we see that as a rebuke for not being generous with our finance, which of course on one level it is. However, I would propose that it is also to consider what we have done and are doing with every gift God has given us.

It is a sobering thought.

On the 22nd of June 2020 during a time of conversation with a friend I heard the Word of the Lord.

He said "Double Up! Double Up! Double Up!"

As I waited I heard this is a time of Double Up. In every area The Lord is saying, "Double Up! Double Up!"

In authority, anointing, revelation, wisdom, healings, miracles, restoration, prosperity, increase, favour, gifting, grace, opportunity, promotion (into our sphere of influence). They were the things that came to me as I pondered. This is not an exhaustive list of things God can and will do, you should insert whatever you are believing for and what Holy Spirit quickens to you at the time.

I also believe the Lord said as you keep decreeing that thing it will continue to be released. Just as in the story of the widow with the empty pots the oil kept pouring as long as there were empty pots to fill.

> *'Now a woman of the wives of the sons of the prophets cried out to Elisha, saying, "Your servant my husband is dead, and you know that your servant feared the LORD; and the creditor has come to take my two children to be his slaves." So Elisha said to her, "What shall I do for you? Tell me, what do you have in the house?" And she said, "Your servant has nothing in the house except a jar of oil." Then he said, "Go, borrow containers elsewhere for yourself, empty containers from all your neighbors—do not get too few. Then you shall come in and shut the door behind you and your sons, and pour into all these containers; and you shall set aside what is full." So she left him and shut the door behind her and her sons; they began bringing the containers to her, and she poured the oil. When the containers were full, she said to her son, "Bring me another container." But he said to her, "There are no more containers." Then the oil stopped. So she came and told the man of God. And he said, "Go, sell the oil and pay your debt, and you and your sons can live on the rest."' 2 Kings 4:1-7 (NASB)*

As I have kept on decreeing the Double Up! I find I am decreeing different areas on different days.

I did enquire of the Lord why I wasn't decreeing the things people usually do for example finance or healing. He said to me that they were the result of what I was decreeing and would automatically flow.

I would encourage you, do not have a ceiling on the goodness of God. He is limitless ! So if we don't stop believing and decreeing, He won't stop delivering.

Let me just add as a caution it is paramount that the believing, the living faith we have in God and His promises accompanies the decree we make. I believe we must absolutely watch over our mouth and the words that we release but words alone may not shift things. As we make faith filled decrees inspired by heaven things happen.

We are in a time, an era, an epoch of increase and accelerated increase.

This is a time of deep calling to deep, the deep things that were birthed in us long ago will now suddenly happen.

> 'Long ago I prophesied things that would happen. I issued decrees and made them known. Then suddenly, I acted and made them happen.'

Isaiah 48:3 (TPT)

Get ready for the suddenlies' of God! Those long held dreams, desires and prophecies that you have almost given up on - "Oh well, it would have been good if it had happened."

Dust them off, start to believe again that they are the Word of God and His Word does not return to Him void, it always accomplishes what it is sent forth to do.

Don't let the Word fall to the ground and die. God is watching over His Word, are you?

We are encouraged to passionately press on to the abundance of what God has called us to. An important key as we look at Philippians 3:12-16 is in verse 13, that we forget all that is past and fasten our hearts and hope to the future. The past whether good bad or indifferent can anchor us. Even if it were a good thing, the past good can colour our future. It is imperative that we remember; God is doing a new thing every day in every way (see Isaiah 43:18-19).

CHAPTER 11

So What's My Mountain?

What is your sphere of influence? Everyone has at least one. I don't believe we should restrict ourselves to just one. As God created us to create we should do that. Pray, and wait on the Lord and He will give you a spark of passion for an area you may never have considered.

The revelation that the early church, the first church understood was that we are the church. The church is more than and organisation or a building we congregate in. The church is the living, breathing Body of Christ. Wherever we are and whatever we do we are the church.

That does not give licence to forsake fellowship, rather we would have a renewed passion for the church and gathering together. That it would be a joy and a celebration instead of an obligation.

Every sphere of influence is important and necessary. It is culture in its entirety. That is exactly what the early church understood. Unfortunately as the future unfolded we were segregated. We became the clergy or the laity or the religious and the secular. My personal belief is that was never the plan or the intention.

If your Bible says as mine does;

> 'Opening his mouth, Peter said: "I most certainly understand now that God is not one to show partiality, but in every nation the man who fears Him and does what is right is welcome to Him."' Acts 10:34-35 (NASB1995).

Then surely although we have different roles in different areas of influence we each have a very important role in the kingdom. Regardless of what our job or our profession maybe, we are called to first influence our world (our part of it) for Christ.

I know that whilst they may not have the title on the door there are many, many Apostles, Prophets, Evangelists, Teachers and Pastors in each of the mountains of destiny. They are there fulfilling the call of God on their lives. They are out in the harvest field transforming culture.

It is only recently these Warriors for Christ were even being recognised. They have been termed marketplace ministers which would intimate they are less than a church minister. They are not a little lower than what is considered a church minister they simply are called to function in a different part of the vineyard. These men and women are truly heroes as they go about what their Lord has called them to, without recognition just to trust Him and obey.

We are all believers in the Lord Jesus Christ and as such are all ministers of the gospel.

There is a big harvest field and we need as many labourers in as many fields/mountains as possible.

My husband Paul for instance. He is an integral part of our family, he also works with men who have broken relationships and families. That is the Family Mountain.

He runs a Business that has different streams, he is a Media genius and also is a very gifted Apostle.

There's four mountains of influence and he is desiring to assault the Arts and Entertainment Mountain.

It is very possible that you may have more influence than you realise. The next step is to yield it all to God, allow Holy Spirit to guide us and teach us and give an assault strategy, so we are not merely lurking around the foothills. Holy Spirit will guide us on a clear path to our place of destiny.

At this point it is important to note the 'Family Mountain' really undergirds our society. It is never enough to just turn up, we must reflect Christ in all we do. As we have victories in the family mountain, I believe change and opportunities will come in the other areas of influence we touch as we operate from a firm foundation;

> "......as for me and my house, we will serve the Lord." Joshua 24:15 (NASB)

I love the scripture

> 'I can do all things through Christ who strengthens me.' Philippians 4:13 (NKJV)

That says to me as I read and mediate on the Living Word I become more and more who He is. As we assimilate the elements by faith during communion we receive Him.

That strengthens us as His life flows through us.

Praying in tongues in the Holy Spirit, scripture says it builds us up, it strengthens us in our spirit man.

> 'But you, beloved, building yourselves up on your most holy faith, praying in the Holy Spirit,'

Jude 1:20 (NASB)

These things are very simple and we can all do them everyday. It is a fallacy that you can only share communion at a church service as it is administered by a minister.

> *'But you are a chosen generation, a royal priesthood, a holy nation, His own special people, that you may proclaim the praises of Him who called you out of darkness into His marvelous light.' 1 Peter 2:9 (NKJV)*

We are all Kings and Priests, a royal priesthood, so if we are believers we also need to be doers.

Meditate on the Word, let the Lord give you new revelation daily, fresh manna daily. Share communion at home with your family and friends as well as in church and pray in tongues, the language of heaven often and see those mountains move!

Okay so we've prayed, met with God and have an inkling or perhaps an absolute surety as to which mountain is ours for the taking.

So what now?

This is the time to forcefully advance in prayer.

> *'And from the days of John the Baptist until now the kingdom of heaven suffers violence, and the*

violent take it by force.' Matthew 11:12 (NKJV)

Unfortunately in amongst the truth of this revelation we have become so familiar with the weight of community opinion. That which stands against us ready to berate us if we are not politically correct. The fear of that may lead to misreading the scriptures to suit that narrative.

I believe God is saying, "Go after the things I have set out for you." Not just go after them like a Sunday afternoon drive - we'll go where the road takes us and if we happen upon our pre-ordained place well - awesome.

You could realistically wander around for many days weeks, or years and never accidentally collide with your destiny.

We need to fix our eyes on what God has promised do not divert, do not detour and don't stop until we get there. Really go after it with passion!

Be aware that as soon as we set out on God's destiny course for our lives there will be obstacles, road blocks distractions which often come from those closest to us. Not because they are evil or don't want the best for us. It is more likely they do not understand and are trying to save us from hurt.

Of course there are also demonic interferences as

the enemy always desires to thwart God's plans.

Those Interferences deserve our most focussed response as we speak and decree with the hosts of heaven all around us ready to carry out what we have decreed, spoken, prophesied.

The more we are one with the Lord, one flesh as His bride, His DNA is flowing through us and therefore His authority. That was why Jesus could completely confidently state; " Behold I have given you authority to tread upon serpents and scorpions, and over all the power of the enemy and nothing shall injure you."

Please note that is not because we speak something and then use the tag line "In Jesus' name". It is because as the Bride of Christ we have His delegated authority. Just as a wife in the natural can speak on behalf of her husband.

It is because we are one with Him, no principality or power can see where the delineation between us is - because there isn't one.

My desire for every believer is as we stand before people they no longer see us they only see Christ.

That's when mountains move. That's when they tremble and shudder at our very presence because they only see Him.

CHAPTER 12

Mountain Moving Prayer

We all want our prayers to be heard and acted upon from The Throne of Grace however, too often our prayers have not had the desired result. That maybe due to our current perspective, but we need to see ourselves as seated in heavenly places with Jesus. When we see ourselves coming from that place we are above the circumstances and our divine authority is released.

The most important point about prayer is our heart has to be right, there can be no doubt or unbelief (Mark 11:23). The door to those things may be opened because of unforgiveness, bitterness and/or resentment. These areas put a wall up between us and God. Disappointment is another thing we can hold onto when things don't go the way we hoped, planned or dreamed they would.

So the first stop for us before praying should always be checking ourselves, then, repenting and returning to the path of righteousness. Please note that I am not preaching from my ivory tower of perfection. Things do get under your skin that's life. What we need to foster is a lifestyle of checking and repenting.

DO IT NOW!

Don't allow things to fester within you as you hold onto something until you need a prayer answered. The thing that works for me is, I ask Holy Spirit to instantly check me if I'm out of line and then I can (and must) respond right then. It doesn't need to be a long drawn out performance of weeping and wailing, He is as close to your next breath so just do it and it's done.

To me one of the other very important scriptures in regard to prayer is Psalms 103:20.

> *'Bless the LORD, you His angels, Mighty in strength, who perform His word, Obeying the voice of His word!' (NASB)*

This confirms to me that we always prayer in concert with the hosts of heaven. They are waiting to obey the voice of His Word, so as we speak His Word (the scriptures) the angels who are poised ready for action hear the Word and go do it.

I have a funny picture of angels all around us waiting expectantly for something to do and they've been waiting so long in may cases they are no longer standing. They are sitting, relaxing totally disengaged from the process. I said it was a funny picture but the seriousness of it is, the inactivity of the angels assigned to us reflects our inactivity.

Please hear my heart I am not having a go at anyone we can all be like that. Remembering what I said earlier, He, Holy Spirit is as close as our next breath. All we have to do is repent and return.

There is a cautionary verse in Psalms 103:15

'Our days are so few, and our momentary beauty so swiftly fades away!' (TPT)

That word for beauty also means shining.

It is well accepted (whether it is correct or not) that beautiful people have more influence. What I am alluding to is Shining in the context of Isaiah 60:1.

"Arise, shine; for your light has come, And the glory of the LORD has risen upon you." (NASB)

We are commanded to arise and shine for your light has come. We know that Jesus is our light and He is in us as we are hidden in Him. It is not just going to continually happen because you gave your life to Jesus sometime ago.

We have the choice to shine or not. We are the shining ones and verse 3 states

> *"Nations will come to your light, And kings to the brightness of your rising." Isaiah 60:3* (NASB)

The world, our sphere of influence will be attracted to us. We just have to take it by faith, just believe. We can change the course of history we can take our place of destiny on our appointed mountain or mountains.

To support and encourage you I have included some scriptures pertaining to the individual mountains.

Please note this is not an exhaustive list and if you have your own and they're hitting the mark use them.

Also remember the Lord is giving fresh revelation everyday and at any point be open to new scripture revelation. We all need every weapon available in our arsenal. An important note is that when something worked once don't make a doctrine don't stop and build a temple to it. The next stage of the assault on your mountain may require completely different tactics and weaponry.

Scriptures to pray into Seven Mountains of Influence

Religion

> Exodus 33:15-16
> Isaiah 2:2
> Jeremiah 9:23-24
> Matthew 16:24
> John 3:16-17
> Romans 12:1-2
> Philippians 4:8-9
> Ephesians 3:14-19
> Jeremiah 29:11-14
> Matthew 6: 9-13

Arts & Entertainment

> 1 Chronicles 25:1
> 2 Chronicles 5:11-14
> Ecclesiastes 2:24
> Psalms 92:1

Family

> Psalms 68:5-6
> Malachi 4:5-6
> Ephesians 5:22,25; 6:2-3
> Isaiah 59:21
> Psalms 78:3-7

Psalms 92:12-15

Business

Deuteronomy 8:18
Psalms 90:17
Haggai 2:6-9
Luke 16:13
Colossians 3:23-25
1 Timothy 6:10
1 Chronicles 4:10
1 Kings 12:7
Deuteronomy 25:13-15
1 Timothy 6:17-19

Education

Exodus 31: 3-5
Psalms 119: 66
Proverbs 7:4
1 Timothy 1:5
Proverbs 22:6
Proverbs 4:5-8
Romans 12:2

Government

Proverbs 29:2
Isaiah 9:6-7
Romans 13:1-4
1 Timothy 2:1-4

Deuteronomy 1:13, 15-17

Media

Proverbs 25:25
Isaiah 40:9
Isaiah 52:7
Isaiah 61:1
Zechariah 8:16-17
Romans 10:15

CHAPTER 13

Who am I in this?

This opens up a whole new part of this revelation. We've spoken previously about calling to specific mountains/spheres of influence and to assist you in that we've listed some occupations that may assist you in crystallising your focus.

Religion

> Apostle
> Prophet
> Evangelist
> Teacher
> Pastor
> Deacon
> Elder
> Worship Leader
> Psalmist

Arts & Entertainment

Author
Publisher
Editor
Actor
Script Writer
Director
Producer
Professional Sportsman

Business

Business Owner
Director
CEO
Employee

Education

Professor
Teacher
Tutor
Coach
Mentor
Student

Government

Head of State
Politician

　　　　Legislators
　　　　Lobbyist
　　　　Judge
　　　　Lawyer/Barristor

Media

　　　　Editor
　　　　Journalist
　　　　Publisher
　　　　Publicist

Again this is not an exhaustive list it is merely designed to provoke thought.

I would draw your attention to the Religion Mountain please notice it is the Religion not the Church Mountain. We all know there are many systems of belief that acknowledge Christ but do not recognise Him as the Resurrected Son Of God. There are also many that do not acknowledge or recognise Him at all. So there is much work to be done in this area.

Within belief systems we have many that are specifically called to prayer. As believers we call them Watchmen or Intercessors.

I am excited that Watchmen are being recognised again as they were in the scriptures. The point I would make here is God Himself mandates Watchmen with authority to pray into certain spheres of influence that they personally may not operate in. This is an extremely important way that we as a body of believers can fulfil Ephesians 4:15-16.

> *'but speaking the truth in love, we are to grow up in all aspects into Him who is the head, that is, Christ, from whom the whole body, being fitted and held together by what every joint supplies, according to the proper working of each individual part, causes the growth of the body for the building up of itself in love.'* (NASB)

Every joint supplying. (Always remembering we are all called to pray regardless of where we believe we are called to.)

We don't all have to be called to any of the other mountains but we are called to support those who are.

This is a stunning picture of the Kingdom forcefully advancing.

I have used the word influence many times I do not shy away from that, as it is not about an influence that is yours or mine, it is only about the ever expanding influence of the Kingdom of Heaven on the Earth.

As that revelation permeates through every cell of our being we will take our place upon the mountain of our calling and no obstacle will stand in our way!

CHAPTER 14

Why Do I Get To Talk About This?

The short answer to that probing question is because God told me to. Now that is not a glib answer just to satisfy the question it is a real urging from the Lord.

As I have pondered the subject I considered where I have staked my claim in terms of mountains of influence.

So currently these are the four mountains I have influence in. There is a fifth you will see that I am currently assailing.

Whilst in some views these are all separate stand alone entities there are things that are common to all so there maybe some cross over.

In the natural if you are a mountain climber (which full disclosure I am not) there are certain disciplines which are common to any assault on a mountain. We can therefore use the lessons learned on one to expedite our ascent on another. Nothing is ever wasted, learn the skills and learn them well.

Religion

I was born into a family of church planters and revivalists on my Mum's side. Obviously as a child I was brought up in church and attended an Anglican/Episcopal school. I understood scripture as a child and received visions and had knowings (words of knowledge) of things as a child I could not possibly have known.

This was in the land of my birth England in the 60s and that landscape was extremely traditional and the things of the Spirit were not spoken of or experienced at large and certainly not by a girl child.

What I did have a belief of was most certainly Jesus.

God the Father was like the words of the hymn Immortal, Invisible. There is a line in that hymn that encapsulated my childlike understanding of God.

'In light inaccessible, hid from our eyes.'

God was inaccessible!

As I grew He become Jehovah Jarrah (incidentally I do know it is Jireh), Jarrah being an Australian hardwood. This was indeed confirming the reality in my mind that God was inaccessible. The Father was in heaven just waiting to catch me out so he could actuate punishment.

I did not doubt my salvation, that came later because I believed as a child my heritage assured me of my place in heaven.

It was painful to discover I was so wrong. This revelation caused me to search out who I was in Christ and who He was in me.

The short version, as I yielded to Holy Spirit He graciously honed the gifts that were given to me before the foundation of the earth and as the parable of the talents tells us, as I used the ones given He gave me more. Please note He is still giving to us all.

I came from a family of preachers on Mum's side and that was what I loved. I wanted to inspire not just the church but anyone. That no matter where they currently were in life, there was always more and better.

Not to leave my Dad's side of the family out, the classic hymn 'What a friend we have in Jesus' was written by Joseph Scriven who was a great, great uncle of my dad's. (not sure how many greats)

I often say to people who tell me they are called to preach however, no one will give them a pulpit so they are just sitting on the sidelines (if you do that for too long you only become bitter not better).

This was my experience, preach to whoever is before you. The manna I received fresh in my time with Lord would miraculously be exactly what the people I was encountering needed. I truly have preached many mo messages out of the pulpit than in it.

I honed my skill. After all what is preaching other than sharing the Good News of Jesus

I was recognised as a Prophet and I say recognised because I was just doing it long before anyone apart from the Lord acknowledged it.

My Husband and I have pastored and planted churches and since 2013 have run Integrity Restoration Ministries which is an Apostolic Hub. There we have opportunity to equip and release ministers into all the seven mountains.

That's where we have planted our flag.

Business

I have always had a love for business, the psychology and mechanics of the discipline, and most importantly the way business influences our society.

It is not about a love of money. God is not against you having stuff, he is against stuff having you. That is what we must always guard against. As we look at the patriarchs in scripture Abraham, Issac, Jacob, Job, and Boaz to name a few. They were wealthy businessmen. Their wealth was completely yielded to God, and the Father used them mightily to influence culture.

In my own right I have owned and operated several extremely successful bookshops around Australia employing and influencing many people. My husband Paul and I since 2013 have run a marketing business with mixed success as our focus has often been elsewhere. God has recently breathed new strategies into us and you can see even in 2020 as we have endured the CoVid isolation the business God has given us is growing.

In regard to business we have always Tithed from the business not simply what we drew from the business.

One day God challenged me as I was preparing the quarterly tax.

He very quietly pointed out to me the tax I was paying to the Government was essentially a tithe so why was I not honouring Him in the same way.

So from that day we did. I won't say it was easy, in my experience nothing worthwhile ever is.

The testimony is God is continuing to increase us daily.

So on the business mountain we are not yet at the place God has prepared for us but we are definitely on the way and along this path we have opportunity to bless and influence so many people. Some who have never met Christ and others who have fallen away under the pressure of life.

Media

This is a very hotly contested mountain. It is a hard mountain and the deception of this age is anyone who has a smart phone can be a YouTube influencer.

The thing about Media is that it is used to communicate News. This is the stronghold of the prince of the power of the air (Ephesians 2:2). As you read that verse it says

> *'in which you previously walked according to the course of this world, according to the prince of the power of the air, of the spirit that is now working in the sons of disobedience.' Ephesians 2:2 (NASB)*

As we read that in context we can see that due to the fall of Adam we were previously under that influence. Now however, it is those who do not yield to Christ who are sons of disobedience, whom the enemy works through today.

You can see this a very hostile environment. The most important thing and something my friend Adrian Beale reminded me of was in Genesis 1:26;

> *'Then God said, "Let Us make mankind in Our image, according to Our likeness; and let them rule over the fish of the sea and over the birds of the sky (heavens) and over the livestock and over all the earth, and over every crawling thing that crawls on the earth."'* (NASB)

It seems very clear to me that the birds of the sky/heavens are the agents of the prince of the power of the air/satan. We have dominion, rule, and authority over them.

These are the current ruling spirits on the Media Mountain. So if you are on this mountain please make sure you are called and then we will take this thing together.

Patricia King once said to us as we were beginning firestartersTV this was the sphere that was the biggest battle.

We are so grateful to her for that honesty as we contend for every foothold on our way to destiny.

No it is not easy but it is so worth it!

Family

My mum and grandmother were very powerful watchmen. They watched over the family in ways I did not. I wanted to be out fighting the big battles secure in the knowledge they were watching and praying for the family.

> *'..then I stationed men in the lowest parts of the space behind the wall, the exposed places, and I stationed the people in families with their swords, spears, and bows. When I saw their fear, I stood and said to the nobles, the officials, and the rest of the people: "Do not be afraid of them; remember the Lord who is great and awesome, and fight for your brothers, your sons, your daughters, your wives, and your houses."' Nehemiah 4:13-14 (NASB)*

This scripture has always been a very clear visual to me of the power and influence of the family group and the watchmen. Working with one hand to rebuild the walls whilst the other holds a weapon.

As I said the picture was very clear to me as I watched my mum and grandmother guard the walls.

Interesting note - they were rebuilding the walls of Jerusalem, symbolically Jerusalem can represent the church, the body of Christ.

I don't believe it is simply representative of a denomination or organisation. I believe it is us. We are the living stones that Holy Spirit is putting in place. Strengthening us, clearing out the rubbish so we can withstand the attacks of the enemy.

When my Grandma went to glory my Mum seamlessly took up her mantle also. Looking back I am sure there were many times she would have loved for me to come and hold her arms up and I am sad to say I never did.

When my Mum passed on to glory the most interesting thing happened and there was no thought process around it. I just assumed that role, if I had thought about I probably would have justified why I was not the person for this job. Yet here I was, and an extraordinary thing happened, God gave me revelation of family from His perspective from his Fathers heart.

The fact that family was the basis of everything. Therefore family was the strength or weakness of everything.

I contended for family in a way I had never considered previously.

Now in fact for those who know me well they have heard me say many times from the platform and in private - they are my family because that is my standpoint. We are so much more than just friends or fellow believers we are family.

Family loves unconditionally whereas with friends it may be conditional and even geographical. My Mum used to call them fair weather friends - that's conditional. There's an old movie called "Romancing the Stone" and the theme of the title song is "When the going gets tough, the tough get going!" I often laughed at that as those who see themselves as tough, mentality, physically, emotionally often do get going but in the other direction.

So I say all this to say I'm on my journey up the family mountain. I believe I am getting better at it as I allow God to permeate every cell of my body, every part of my soul and consciously yield my spirit.

So currently these are the four mountains I have influence in.

You may have more, you may have less but remember always we are one body. It is not a competition it is a collaboration.

Right now having completed my first two published works. I am in the process of writing this book with several others at various stages of development. I have always had a passion for the written word. My Dad's father was a journalist! I am excited to explore the world of literature. So I am just setting off up the

Arts and Entertainment Mountain.

There is no limit in God, nothing is impossible to Him so I strike out in His strength.

CHAPTER 15

From Here To There

Two questions spring to mind in regard to this and every other revelation or doctrine:

Where do I fit?

How do I get there?

My answer to you is simple yet often difficult.

Get before the Lord, wait on Him until He reveals the roadmap to you. Sometime He only reveals the very next step, often times it may seem a very circuitous route, one of the big lessons in our life with Christ is to trust the process.

I often hear people say, "Oh God is just testing us" when from our prayer to our answer is not the A to

B route we imagined. That response troubles me it's kind of as though God needs to be let off the hook for not answering prayer. Or perhaps being slow to respond - my reply to that is God is not on a coffee break! Or maybe we just didn't like His answer and are waiting for another one.

This is my response that during this time from where I am at until I receive my promise or answer I am seeking, the Lord is building me (not testing) so that I become the person that can hold that answer to prayer. To stand in that place of destiny that the Lord has prepared for me before the foundation of the earth.

Tests can be failed and God will not set you up to fail - He loves you!

Holy Spirit knows us better than we know ourselves He knows where we've been and where we're going . To that end He knows the best path for us. He wants to ensure when we reach our destined place we are fully equipped. He is invested in our success and victory, that we are moving in the full authority of heaven, with great love and wisdom. Most importantly we are able to stand in that place because we have allowed Holy Spirit to develop us. We will not fall off the mountain.

If you feel like the heavens are brass, perhaps a fast

may be required. That can clear the lines of communication very swiftly.

As a matter of course pray in tongues, learn the discipline. Commune with heaven in your heavenly language it is awesome.

Never rule anything out, don't limit the yearning of the Father's heart to speak to you.

There is a lot to be said for vulnerability. It is not weakness, no one achieves anything in isolation there is always a team. After all we are the 'body of Christ'.

I heard a wise man say this "For you to get what you want, just help other people get what they want."

Just because God has usually communicated with you in a certain way, never think that is the only way He will communicate with you.

Be open to new and exciting adventures in the Spirit always ensure that things line up with the Spirit breathed Word of God.

As we embark upon a journey scaling our mountain of destiny consider this; as you climb a mountain in the Spirit it is not dissimilar to climbing a mountain in the natural.

If for instance we were planning to climb a significant peak such as Everest or Kilimanjaro we would most certainly prepare and train. We would be prepared for the rigours of the climb and also for any unexpected occurrences perhaps accidents along the way. We would be well equipped with all the supplies we would need for these often treacherous journeys. Yet it occurs to me that as we embark on a 'spiritual Mountain climb' we are often ill prepared for such an undertaking. We are in such a hurry to get to the peak we forsake the necessary training for haste. We have some strange idea that because these mountains these spheres of influence are in the natural world perhaps spiritual training is not as necessary. Trust me when I say do not neglect the training of your spirit man.

So how do we train? We do all the simple things! We pray in tongues building up our spirit man, we read the word and seek revelation from Holy Spirit we build up our faith muscles.

The gifts of the spirit are very important as we undertake the task before us. So it's important that we would be well practised. The gifts of the spirit can prevent us falling into a spiritual abyss.

As we train and build ourselves for the task ahead a major key to remember is that we are here for such a time as this. We are in this world but we are not of this world. We are of heaven. We are ambassadors sent on behalf of heaven to change to transform the culture on this earth.

We are the ecclesia and as such it was always our call, our mandate to transform culture. To bring Heaven to Earth and to do that in which ever unique way God has gifted us. And we will all do that in differing spheres of influence.

At this point it's really important to wait upon the Lord if you haven't already done so, as to where do you fit? Which sphere do you have influence in? And if you are influential in one area is that where God wants you to stay? Do you have influence on another mountain? Do you have the ability and the desire to move into that as well?

The Elevator Dream

I don't dream prolifically so when I do it arrests me and I really want to know what Holy Spirit is saying to me.

I found myself in a freight elevator in what seemed like a warehouse.

There were some other people in the elevator, though not many and they were not familiar to me.

The thing that struck me as we ascended was the elevator doors were open. Normally I would have been concerned about that however, in the dream I wasn't. As we stopped at each floor people got off until only I remained. Eventually we reached the top and the dream ended.

The dream seemed quite pertinent to the context of mountain destiny, although I had not fully discerned the meaning.

I shared the dream with my friend Adrian Beale (co-author of The Divinity Code to Understanding Dreams and Visions) and he offered me some very interesting insights; firstly as it was a freight elevator which carries heavy goods the Lord was showing me I was carrying something very weighty.

In regard to the open doors he felt this spoke to the fact that as I went up it would be public, on show as it were.

The other people leaving on different floors wasn't a negative it was just that they had reached their place, their destiny, whereas I was riding it as far as it went.

As we have said previously the summit isn't necessarily our destiny and that's not negative. We should all desire to fulfil our potential and reach our place of destiny.

Another thought I had about this dream was the people who had left at lower floors could perhaps get back on and come up at another time.

I was greatly encouraged by this dream and saw the Father had not only made a way for me, but a direct route to destiny.

This is the time to springboard into your place of destiny on your mountain of influence.

This is the time to stand before your mountains and see them shudder and melt before you as the presence, anointing and authority of heaven you carry is evidenced.

This is the time to forcefully advance the kingdom as we take inspiration from Caleb and run up our mountains. Never seeing them as negative. If the mountain is an obstacle as in Mark 11:22-24, we have faith and power through Christ to see it go. If on the other hand it is a mountain or sphere of influence, let's be like Caleb excited at the prospect of scaling it and conquering any resident principalities as in Joshua 14:6-12.

So I want to encourage everyone who reads this, no matter where you have started your destiny awaits. As I have said many times as believers in Christ we have all enlisted in the Army of God, that make us all servants that is ministers. So regardless of the place of our influence we are ministers in our place. Let's play our part allowing Holy Spirit to flow through us fulfilling our destiny call.

End notes

1. Sir Edmund Hilary - Wikipedia

2. Reinhold Messner - Wikipedia

   Mount Everest
   On 8 May 1978, Reinhold Messner and Peter Habeler reached the summit of Mount Everest; the first men known to climb it without the use of supplemental oxygen. Prior to this ascent it was disputed whether this was possible at all. Messner and Habeler were members of an expedition led by Wolfgang Nairz along the southeast ridge to the summit. Also on this expedition was Reinhard Karl, the first German to reach the summit, albeit with the aid of supplemental oxygen.

   Two years later, on 20 August 1980, Messner again stood atop the highest mountain in the world, without supplementary oxygen. For this solo climb, he chose the northeast ridge to the summit, where he crossed above the North Col in the North Face to the Norton Couloir and became the first man to climb through this steep gorge to the summit. Messner decided spontaneously during the ascent to use this route to bypass the exposed northeast ridge. Prior to this solo ascent, he had not set up a camp on the mountain.

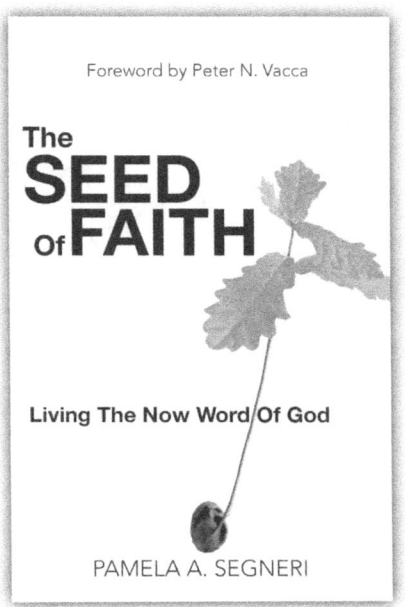

Faith is perhaps the simplest and most difficult discipline we ever have to master. I love that old saying, "from little acorns great oak trees grow". Those acorns are a metaphorical representation of our seed of faith. From those humble seed beginnings we grow and become all that we can be in God.

This is written to inspire and encourage.

The Seed of Faith…. it is in you!

www.theseedoffaithbook.com

ABOUT THE AUTHOR

Pamela Segneri is the co-founder of Integrity Restoration Ministries Inc and the co-founder and Host of firestartersTV. Her desire is to see you fulfil your God given destiny.

www.integritygroup.org.au

www.firestartersTV.com.au

www.ingramcontent.com/pod-product-compliance
Lightning Source LLC
Chambersburg PA
CBHW050318010526
44107CB00055B/2290